Bruce H

In Pursuit of

the Aha! &

Ha! hA! Ha!

Games & activities that support, challenge and use creative and divergent thinking in the classroom

**More than 90 fun
Games & Activities for
CHALLENGING & EXPANDING
Student's
Creativity,
Imagination
Problem Solving,
and Critical Thinking**

For ages 6 and up

Dedicated to Seth

Honig, Bruce.
In Pursuit of the Aha and Ha Ha Ha! for Teachers:
Games & activities that support, challenge and use creative and divergent thinking in the classroom

Summary
More than 90 fun games & activities for challenging & expanding children's creativity, imagination, problem solving, and critical thinking

Contact for Comments and More Information
Honig IdeaGuides
www.ideaguides.com
bruce@ideaguides.com

TABLE OF CONTENTS

1

Creating Words & Stories

Perceiving is believing...believing is perceiving

Theorizing/Speculating

Curiosity will never kill the cat...only your spirit

The future is today

That makes reasonable sense

36 Additional Activities

Resources for More Information & Activities

Order this Book

Feedback

Author

PREFACE

The games and activities in this book have two purposes:
1) to have fun, and 2) to use and exercise one's most
valuable resource: creativity. It is my intention that you
use this book like you would a recipe book, putting
together a menu of activities to use in your curriculum. It
can be applied to most any subject: writing, science,
history, civic studies, social studies, current events, any
subject that requires creative thinking

Most of these game can be played with any number of
student. Keep in mind that it is critical that you give all
your students equal opportunity during the play of the
games. Some of the games and activities are to be played
by two people. For these you can put your student into
pairs. Enjoy!!

CREATIVITY IS...

the process of exploring and creating new territory in order to accomplish a goal.

Creative Children...

- Create new patterns of thinking

- Understand and appreciate complexities

- Keep options open as long as possible

- Suspend judgment initially

- Think broadly, and see many relationships & connections

- Break out of habits

- Attempt to see things differently than others

- Use personal strategies to generate & solve problems

Your creative students needs and wants...

- 🖐 To explore new ideas and make new discoveries

- 🖐 To meet challenges and to attempt difficult tasks

- 🖐 To give him/herself completely to a task

- 🖐 To be an individual

- 🖐 To be honest and search for the truth

...in order to continue being creative.

All children (people) are creative!

BLUEPRINT FOR ENCOURAGING CREATIVITY

70 things you can do to support your child's creativity

1   Provide materials that enrich imagery such as stories, myths and fables, and art

2   Permit time for thinking and daydreaming

3   Encourage your students to record his/her ideas in a scrapbook or tape recorder

4   Encourage your students to look at things from different perspectives

5   Praise rather than punish true individuality

6   Allow and encourage your students to ask questions

7   Recognize that your students are creative

8   Provide problems to solve and decisions to make that have meaning to your students

9   Avoid <u>constant</u> evaluation of behavior, positive or negative

10   Emphasize internal rewards over external rewards (focus on self-gratification over reaching the carrot)

11   De-emphasize competition in play

12   Encourage your students' own individual talents

13   Urge your students to accept his/her limitations

14   Invite making use of opportunities when they arise

15   Encourage your students to develop values and purpose

16   Stress the importance of holding to purpose

17   Reduce emphasis on sex roles/cultural roles

18   Encourage fears, hardships and failure to be dealt with

19   Allow your students to feel and accept ambiguity and uncertainty, and assure him/her that it is perfectly normal

20   Encourage your student to go beyond the obvious

21   Ask your students to elaborate on drawing, stories, etc.

22   Encourage the experimentation and testing of ideas

23   Encourage the synthesizing of diverse and apparently irreverent elements.

24   Prepare your students for new experiences

25   Emphasize progress rather than punishment

26 Provide your students with opportunities to make a contribution to the classroom, school and to society

27 Encourage learning from a variety of different resources

28 Encourage developing new interests

29 Allow your student to say "I don't know" without ridicule

30 Ask your students for opinions

31 Invite your students to think about ideas

32 Ask students to be involved in decision making

32 Ask your students thought provoking questions

33 Look at mistakes as a place to learn, rather than a reason to punish

34 Provide your students with a variety of different games (board, computer etc.)

35 Urge your students to become committed to his/her task

36 Allow your kids to think about and explore new ideas and new subjects

37 Ask your students not to jump too quickly to conclusions, but to first explore options.

38   Admit that you often do not have the truth or answer (practice saying, "I don't know)

39   Teacher, remember your own child that lives inside you.

40   Encourage the students to be a child and not "grow up"

41   Praise your students often

42   Encourage independence

43   Allow your students to express all feelings (constructively), including anger

44   Expose your students to different values

45   Allow your students to question your decisions

46   Plan for spontaneity with your students, don't always structure class work

47   Share your own interests

48   Allow your students the freedom to make his/her own decisions

49   Respect your students' efforts to be him/herself.

50   Appreciate your students' creative activity

51   Respect your students' opinions and encourage him/her to express them

52   Favor values over rules

53   Encourage the need to achieve and improve (as oppose to making good grades)

54   Appreciate all types of creative activity and expressions, not just certain types of art, but also finding business solutions, cooking, tour and party planning, making people happy...etc.

55   Tell your students s/he is creative

56   Don't pressure your students

57   Allow your students to take "reasonable" risks (physical and intellectual)

58   Create a vision of your students being the great creative person they are

59   Help your students search for answers

60   Allow your students to answer his/her own questions first, then help with the answer, if needed

61   Encourage your students to figure things out

62   Discourage your students to do things because you like them, encourage him/her do things because they like them

63   Openly tell jokes; laugh

64   Have fun with the games and activities in this book and do them frequently

65   Follow the general rules for playing the games in this book (on the following page) in your life with your students daily.

66   Encourage your students to use his/her imagination

67   Provide interesting things to look in the classroom

68   Provide students with paints, crayons and crafts supplies

69   Suggest new and different activities to do

70   Remember that you are an important model for your students... Do all of the above for yourself as well.

PLAYING THE GAMES

General Rules for these games
(and all of life)

For the games and activities that follow, we urge you to adapt them or change them to make them work for you and your students. However, there are a few rules that ought not to be broken:

Rule #1   Encourage a variety of responses
🖐 Accept all responses. There are no "right" or "wrong" answers.
🖐 Invite many different alternative responses.

Rule #2   Encourage original responses
🖐 Encourage your **students** to create ideas that no one else will think of
🖐 Encourage uniqueness

Rule #3   Encourage quantity of responses
🖐 Ask for as many ideas as possible
🖐 Always ask for an increase in ideas, just a little beyond the limit of your **students**.

Rule #4   Encourage specific responses
🖐 Ask probing questions, such as: "What else could it be?" "How else could you do it?" "What would happen if?" "Explain further." "What do you mean by?"

Rule #5   Understand how to play the game
🖐 Read through each activity before beginning the activity or game to avoid confusion and frustration.

Rule #6   Don't require your students to answer or play the games. They should be able to "pass" at any time.

GAMES

BUILDING A BETTER MOUSETRAP

Improving everyday objects using one's greatest resource: imagination

Step #1   Choose an object (best for the adult to start).

Step #2   Ask: "**How can [*the object*] be improved?**"

Step #3   The other players respond with as many answers as they can provide.

Step #4   The next player chooses another object and play continues as above.

Examples of questions

How would you improve a car?

How would you improve a broom?

How would you improve a pencil sharpener?

How would you improve comic books?

Hints

You do not have to go far to find objects to improve.

Just look around where you are right now.

You may notice a table, a chair, a bed, even the wall.

These are all items that are fine to use for this game.

Everything can be improved!

INVENTING OVER EASY

Invention usually comes from a need...mostly to make things easier—After all necessity is the Mother of Invention

Step #1   Pick any subject matter or situation

Step #2   Ask a student: "**What would you invent to make (the subject matter or situation) easier?**"

Step #3   The student responds with as many solutions as possible

Step #4   Have that student ask another student another (or the same) inventing question.

Examples

What would you invent to make SCHOOL easier

What would you invent to make LIFE easier for the homeless and poor?

What would you invent to make PEOPLE GET ALONG WITH EACH OTHER?

What would you invent to make BASEBALL easier for people who find it hard to hit a regular ball?

Hints

Don't feel restricted to the sentence form written above. Also, you do not have to use the word "easier." Other words you can use are:

* Cheaper
* Faster
* Slower
* More attractive
* More interesting
* More fun
* Smaller
* Tastier
* Smarter

TRANSFORMING THE OBJECT
A method for creating new product ideas

Step #1   Either you or a student picks any object.

Step #2   Have your students think of a list of 6 verbs that will modify an object, such as, expand, reduce or divide. And assign each verb with a unique number from 1-6.

Step #3   Get a die you may have around the house. Roll the die. Make note of the number which corresponds to the number on the die and the verb number, i.e. If you role a 3 then you pick verb 3. (Alternatively you can have a student close his/her eyes and point to one.)

Step #4   Have your students use your imagination to modify/change/improve the chosen object based on the selected modifying verb. Explain or/and draw what it looks like and what it can be used for.

Modifying Verbs

* Shorten it
* Reverse it
* Rearrange it
* Change it
* Lower it
* Divide it
* Add it
* Decrease it
* Adapt it
* Distort it
* Hang it
* Cushion it
* Loosen it

Hints

When using the modifying verb, think of the many ways that the word can imply. For example, shorten can mean to make smaller or to make faster (shorten time), or to make it more compact, etc.

MAKING IT WITH 4
Combine ordinary objects to make a sculptor

Step #1 Have your students go through the classroom and make note of four common objects.

Step #2 Have your students combine their own four objects to make anything they please.

Step #3 Once they complete the project, have the students describe what it is and how it works. You can do this too, teacher.

Suggestions for objects

* Paper clip
* Pencil
* String
* Paper
* Flashlight
* Plastic or paper cup
* Bucket
* Old book
* Old clothes
* Soap
* Sponge
* Lock
* Candle

Hints

Be careful not to use any objects that could hurt your child, and that you wish not to damage. Other than that, the sky is the limit for the types of objects.

NEW WAYS TO DO THE OLD
Find new ways to do normal-everyday things

Step #1   Ask a student to either describe or to act out at least five different ways to do something they do ordinarily. Ask, **"What are at least 5 ways to [do the ordinary activity]."**

Step #2   Ask for a volunteer to go next. Ask your volunteer the same question but with a different activity. Continue to ask for volunteers until everyone has had a chance to go.

Ordinary things to use in this activity
* Ways to put on a coat
* Ways to walk across a room
* Ways to brush ones teeth
* Ways to go to school
* Ways to greet people on the phone
* Ways to sleep
* Ways to sneeze
* Ways to hop
* Ways to say "I love you"
* Ways to tell a story
* Ways to eat Chinese food
* Ways to capture a butterfly

USES & USES & USES
Generate many uses for an object

Step #1   Pick an object, most any object.

Step #2   Ask the question, filling in the blank with your selected object, **"In how many ways can you use a [*the object*]?"**

Step #3   Players alternate answering the question, each providing one answer when it is their turn. Do this until you have at least 8 uses.

Objects you can use

* Tin cans
* Paper clips
* Piece of glass
* Old record player
* Toothpick
* Used tires

Example: Uses for old tennis ball:

* Use in a carnival game
* Cut in half to use as a planter
* Cut in half to use to print circles
* Use as protectors on blades
* Make a salt & pepper shaker out of it

Hints

Remember not to evaluate the answers in this activity.

Encourage your child to come up with a variety of different uses. Also encourage the game to last as long as possible. If someone can't think of a use they can pass, do however encourage some response.

WHAT IS A META...PHOR?

Comparing things allows us to find new connections and new attributes

Step #1   Think of two everyday objects.

Step #2   Fill in the blank using your chosen two objects: "**In what ways is a [*the object*] like a [*the other object*]?**" Ask your students this question.

Step #3   Have your students each ask a similar question (with different objects) to the class. Do this as many times as you wish.

Metaphor questions

- In what ways is a shirt like a hair?
- In what ways is a heart like glue?
- In what ways is a clock like a sun?
- In what ways is a cat like an ocean?
- In what ways is a parachute like n eraser?
- In what ways is a banana like a fish?
- In what ways is a globe like a computer?
- In what ways is cotton like a pig?
- In what ways is a train like a blue whale?

Hints

You can play this game with more than two people. With one person providing the question and the others giving one answer each...then switching to a new questioner.

Remember to not criticize the answers.

MAKING CONNECTIONS

A basic trait of creative people: The ability to identify how things relate to one another

Step #1 Think of two everyday objects.

Step #2 Fill in the blank using your chosen two objects: **"What do [the object] and [the other object] have in common?"** Ask your students this question.

Step #3 Have your students each ask a similar question (with different objects) to the class. Do this as many times as you wish.

Examples of Objects

* What do an eraser and a pillow have in common?
* What do a light bulb and a pole have in common?
* What do a rainbow and a tunnel have in common?
* What do a rug and a dress have in common?
* What do a hippopotamus and pants have in common?
* What do a flag, leaf and a brick have in common?
* What do a clown, chair and whale have in common?

Hints

To make this game a little more difficult you can use three objects. However, any more than three will make it extremely difficult.

You can play this game with several people. With one person providing the question and the others giving one different answer each...then switching to a new questioner.

For younger kids, use objects that have more obvious connections, such as a pen and a pencil. But remember to stretch your students's creative muscles.

ABSOLUTELY POSITIVELY

Great ideas usually are born by searching out opportunities in problems and recognizing the good in the bad

Step #1   Choose something that is not pleasant, such as "war".

Step #2   Ask your students to state at least one good thing about this unpleasant thing. Use this form: "**What is positive about [*the nasty thing*]."**

Step #3   Have your students each ask a similar question (with different nasty thing) to the class. Do this as many times as you wish.

Looking at the positive

* Name 3 good things about doing homework.
* Name 3 good things about war.
* Name 3 good things about getting robbed.
* Name 3 good things about your TV not working.
* Name 3 good things about getting lost in a foreign country.
* Name 3 good things about having a broken finger.
* Name 3 good things about being in the rain without an umbrella.

Hints

Use any object or subject that you believe the player views to be negative.

Remember not to judge the answers. For example, If your student says that the best thing about having a broken finger is not having to write any more, accept it as an answer.

Have younger children may choose only one or two things.

WEATHER PERSON
Finding the good in all weather

Step #1   Select a weather condition, and make a statement when you would like that weather to occur.
For example: "I select heavy rains...I want this when I've just built a pond".

Step #2   Have your students do the same in round robin fashion. Do this until you and your students have weathered this game enough.

Ideas for weather conditions

* Earthquake
* Hurricane
* Heavy rain
* -50° (below 0°)
* Blizzard
* Lightning
* Fast winds
* Beautiful, clear

Tips

Encourage your students to develop as many ideas as possible. Also, encourage interesting and unique responses.

Do not judge the responses, naturally some ideas will be better than others. There is no right or wrong answer.

WHAT IN THE *?#?* IS IT?
Making the unusual usual

Step #1   Find some objects that are a little unusual looking (e.g. half of a tennis ball, a piece of a machine that you rarely see, an odd tool, etc.).

Step #2   Pass the objects around, one at a time each person says what they think it is by giving it a name and explaining what it does. The intention is for each person to give a different answer

Hints

Urge the players to not be literal here. The object is not to find what the object really is but to play with it and find new or even funny things that the object could be.

Do not judge the "rightness" or "wrongness" of the answers.

TELL ME... WHAT IS IT?

Describing in detail is a necessary tool for focusing on problems and projects

Step #1   Pick a familiar item or place for your students' to describe. Use an item or place that can be seen at the moment

Step #2   Have your students, one at a time, describe the item or place. Encourage your students to be specific and detailed by asking: "What do you mean by (the statement s/he said)," and "What else can you tell me about the object?"

Step #3   Continue the above for as long as both you and your students are engaged.

Examples of objects you can use

* Telephone

* Bedroom

* The child's toy

* Light bulb

* The home

* Food (a sandwich)

* Coins (a penny)

Hints

Your students will typcially not volunteer specific descriptions. Therefore it is important for you to ask probing questions and summarize your student's response. For example, the object you picked was a penny:

Student: It is round with a President on it.
You: What else is on the penny?
Next Student: a building
You: What kind of building?
Next Student: A big building.
You: What do you mean by big building?
Next Student: Bigger than our house.
You: So, the penny is round with a president and a very big building on it, bigger than our house. Great!

FANTASY STORIES

All creative thoughts start with a fantasy—share yours

Step #1   Make up an original fantasy story and tell the story to your students.

Step #2   Have your students make up and tell you another story, one student at a time.

Types of fantasies

* Something changes in your life.
* How you found something valuable.
* A fantasy about a mythical creature.
* A day in the life of an animal.
* Space-oriented fantasies.
* Flying to mysterious lands.
* How an object mysteriously changed into another object.
* An original story of how the world was created.
* A peaceful fantasy.
* A rock and roll fantasy.
* Being famous.

Hints

Let the stories flow with little judgment and forethought as to where it will go. You will probably surprise yourself with the kind of story you can develop. Also encourage your student to not evaluate his/her own story.

The stories can be as long as you both would like them to be.

You can do this with several people.

SPONTANEOUS THOUGHTS

Encourage the spontaneous thought since it is often the most creative

Step #1 Pick a subject or object.

Step #2 Fill in the blank using your chosen subject or object: "**What is the first thing that comes to your mind when you think of [*the object or subject*]?**"

Step #3 Have every student respond quickly.

Step #4 Then have a student pick a subject or object and continue as above. Do this until all the students had a chance to pick a subject or object.

Objects and subjects

"What is the first thing that comes to your mind when you think of...

* Dogs?"
* Life raft?"
* Hamburger?"
* Little Mermaid?"
* Family?"

Hints

Sometimes it is hard to find objects and subjects. Here are some places to find them: titles of books, names of shows, objects around the house/school, dictionaries and encyclopedias, stores in which you go shopping.

Remember to encourage spontaneity – this is a "stream-of consciousness" activity.

CREATE-A-WORD

Step #1   Make up an entirely new word, perhaps "sqigegly."

Step #2   The other player(s) defines the word using only their creative muscles.

Step #3   Switch roles. Have the each student make up a word and follow steps #1 and #2. Do this as many times as you wish.

Examples of new words

Droot

Loomlies

Fritch

Spewie

Slazz

Imcabitel

Funquetence

Hints

Remember to use an entirely made-up word.

There are no right or wrong definitions when the player in Step #2 defines the word.

WHAT'S IN A NAME?

Find names for things: a exercise for creative thought

Step #1   Pick an imaginary or real product that your students would enjoy.

Step #2   Tell your students what the object is, then have him/her make up a new unique name for it.

Step #3   Switch roles. Have each student pick an imaginary or real product that they would enjoy and follow steps #1 and #2. Do this as many times as you wish.

Objects to rename

What would you name a new thriller carnival ride?

Make up a name for a new chewing gum that taste like mango.

Rename the 7 dwarves.

If you owned a spaceship what would you name it?

What would you name a tree that walks and talks?

What would you name a new medicine that taste good?

What would you name a three-headed lion with seven tails?

Variation

To create a object you can combine two known things, for example:

What would you name a vegetable that is half potato and half tomato?

What would you name an animal that is half monkey and half turkey?

ONCE UPON A TIME
Story-telling where all players tell

Step #1   Make up a line or two that might fit in a story.

Step #2   A student then comes up with the next part of the story. Another student continues.

Step #3   Make sure no one part is too long (five sentences or longer). The story ends whenever someone concludes the story.

Story starts

There was an old man lived in a cottage in a deep forest. He was very lonely. His only companion is a dog. The old man did not know but...

Story Ideas

A myth about how people got 10 fingers.

A table that won a special prize for writing a comic book.

Hints & Variations

You can pick a story about something silly or unusual like a life of a single tooth or something more common like the life of a dog.

MAKE UP A POEM
The verse can be terse, or vice a versa

Step #1	Make up a line or two that might fit into a poem.
Step #2	A student then continues the poem by coming up with the next line. Then another student does the next line. And so on and so forth.
Step #3	Keep the above until you all feel the poem is finished.
Step #4	Have someone name the poem after it is over.

First lines in a poem

Whiggity, wackity to...

There was a girl named flute.

There was a man who met an old witch...

The small man ran...

The flowers warm, and full...

The day is strong...

Hints

The poem does not have to rhyme.

Accept any line, you are not writing a Pulitzer prize poem (on the other hand, who knows?).

YOU CAN'T SAY THAT
Finding alternative words to say

Step #1   Choose two to four common words, such as "Yes", "No", "Black", and "white". (These words will be forbidden to say). Let all players know what words these are.

Step #2   Ask questions to each player one at a time. They must answer and answer truthfully. The goal is to provoke the other player(s) to say the forbidden words. If the answerer says the forbidden word go to the next step (3). Should you be playing with more than two people, continue this round until all but one player is has said the forbidden word.

Step #3   Alternate roles

Be tricky

If the words are "yes" "no," and "white":

Tell a story and ask in the middle of it a yes or no question, like: do you like this story?

Change your tone of voice to a more serious one and ask a yes/no question, like: Are you hungry?

Ask about a color, What color is this (pointing to a white rug)?

Hints

Think of a variety of different questions.

Encourage your studentto think up of new ways to say the same thing.

NAME THINGS THAT ARE...
Naming things that belong to certain categories

Step #1   Think of a general category, such as the color white. (See below for additional examples)

Step #2   A student responds with an item in the category you stated, e.g. Marshmallow.

Step #3   Then, same student states another category and another student thinks of an item that fits into that category.

Step #4   Repeat steps #2 and #3 until you and your students had enough.

Categories

Colors: things that are red, yellow, blue etc.

Furniture

Hard or soft things

Things that require electricity

Things that are made up of a particular material: metal, plastic, glass etc.

Cold or Hot Things.

Old or new things

Zoo Animals

Loud or soft things

Tips/Variation

Instead of one answer (in Step #2), you can require that each player give a certain number of items (perhaps 3 or 5) before they can offer a new category.

Whatever number you choose, make sure that it provides your with just the right amount of challenge (you want them to think hard and stretch, but not be anxious).

To make it harder use two or more categories (e.g. white and soft)

EMOTIONAL ROULETTE
Making sentences

Step #1   On 24 index cards put the following two numbers:

1-3, 1-4, 1-5, 1-6, 2-3, 2-4, 2-5, 2-6, 3-3, 3-4, 3-5, 3-6, 4-3, 4-4, 4-5, 4-6, 5-3, 5-4, 5-5, 5-6, 6-3, 6-4, 6-5, 6-6

(The first number is ranged 1-6, the second is ranged from 3-6.)

The first number represents an emotion
  1 = love,
  2 = fear,
  3 = hate,
  4 = scared,
  5 = joy,
  6 = sadness.
Shuffle the deck.

Step #2   Each person takes turns picking a card and then creating a sentence using the word indicated by the first number and using the number of words indicated by the second number.

Examples

3,6: Hate is on it's way out
5,3: Joy is one
6,3: Refugees of sadness
1,5: When love conquers, there's peace

Additional rules

The sentences do not have to be grammatically correct.

Hints

Encourage your students to not use the same sentence structure over and over again, e.g. I_____you; I really _____you.

Avoid using clichés.

Variation

Change what the first number represents, a different emotion, object or any word..

SILLY SENTENCES
Creating the silly sentence

Step #1   A player starts with a basic beginning part of a sentence, for example "I saw a horse...".

Step #2   Go around so that all players add a silly sentence to go with this perfectly logical sentence, for example "climb the Golden Gate Bridge."

Step #3   Continue till everyone gets a chance to create a beginning sentence

Sentence beginnings

* There in the barn is...
* I was in a shop...
* You can get a...
* The barrel had a thousand...
* I saw a lamb sitting....
* Happy people stop...
* Find one thing that...

Tips

Encourage your students to get as silly as you know they are capable.

Variation

Tell a complete story using the same format.

STORY DANCE

Working together to create a story

Step #1   Either your or a student makes up a title for a story.

Step #2   You begin the story with one word and the next person adds another word, and the next person (you again, if only two people) will continue the story by adding a single word, on and on until the story comes to what seems to be an end. You can change direction in the story but attempt to stay within the bounds of "sense."

Example of a story

The story of it

IT was A little BUG that LIVED in A BIG hole. ONE day IT went OUT to SHOP to BUY new SHELVES for HIS hole. HE didn't HAVE enough MONEY so HE worked FOR the SHELVES by WASHING cars....

(Caps = you, Lower case = your child, if only two players).

Hints

The goal is to make the story seamless, so there are few "uhs," and empty spaces. To help you and students do this, remind your students not to decide what the word is before it is your turn.

Variation

You can do a poem, phrase or advertisement this way.

FANTASY VISIT
Thinking the ordinary in unordinary ways

Step #1   You and your students are visitors from outer space, with different customs, laws, behavior and manners than earth. Your task is to learn about earth and its inhabitants.

Step #2   Talk about your far out planets, customs, laws, behavior and manners.

Step #3   Take a walk around your school together as space creatures and ask naive questions about earth and observe the earthlings.

Things to do as a space-visitor

Sample the strange food & drinks that the earthlings eat.

Go window shopping and notice the odd things that earthlings buy.

Notice the sights (the buildings), the smells (the flowers), and sounds (cars & trucks).

Hints

Your task is to stay in the role of a visitor. Avoid coming out of character.

Show your curiosity and investigate as many things as you both can.

Variation

Pretend that you are each animals. Experience the world from the viewpoint of the animal. Animals: cat, tiger, horse, mule, bear, snake, baboon etc.

Words

INITIALLY
Creating sentences using just initials

Step #1   State 5 letters at random (e.g. T R S J O).

Step #2   All players are to create their own sentence out of these letters.

Step #3   Once this is done, a new person randomly picks five letters.

Step #4   Continue until you all wish to stop.

Examples

F M S D:
For my sake don't

T C B T O
This can't be the only

W D Y T B
What do you think, Buddy?

I L F D M
I like fun dancing music

Tips

You can adjust the ease and challenge of this game by adding or reducing the number of initial letters, and by limiting the letters to the frequent or infrequent used ones.

You can also help each person create their sentence. (But try not to do it for them...it not fun that way).

46

PICTURE THIS (VERSION ONE)
Drawing something from nothing

Step #1   Have each person draw a squiggly line on a sheet of paper.

Step #2   Have each person pass the paper to the person on his or her right (or left – it does not matter).

Step #3   Tell your students to make something out of this line on the new sheet of paper. Keep passing the paper several times.

Step #4   Pass the sheet of paper again and repeat step #3. Pass it 4 or 5 times (or so). Afterwards you can then start with a fresh clean sheet of paper and repeat all the steps.

Squiggles

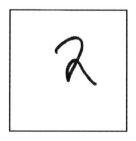

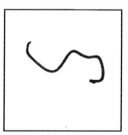

Needs

You will need pieces of paper and a pencil or pen (with colors, preferably).

Hints

It is okay for your students to create an abstract drawing...accept all responses positively.

Art

PICTURE THAT (VERSION TWO)
Drawing something from nothing...together

Step #1   Start by drawing a squiggly line of any shape.

Step #2   Your child then makes only one mark on the same paper using the squiggly line, having something, specific, in mind to create.

Step #3   You then draw another doodle on that sheet using all the doodles, having something, specific, in mind to create.

Step #4   Continue in this manner, going back and forth, each person drawing on the sheet of paper until the drawing is complete.

Squiggles

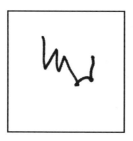

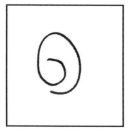

Hint

You can play this with several people at a time, each person contributing to the drawing, all the while attempting to create a picture of something recognizable.

Avoid judging the drawing and making the drawing be what you want it to be. Your players may have something else in mind.

CIRCLE GAME

Drawing as many objects as you can using the same object

Step #1   Draw 20 circles on a piece of paper. (you can draw more or less). Print these up, one sheet per student, and distribute them to your students.

Step #2   Ask your student draws one thing, anything, using one or two circles on the sheet.

Step #3   The students pass the sheet to their left (or right) and repeats Step #2.

Step #4   Continue repeating steps #2-#3 until you fill up the sheet circles are filled up

Circle drawings

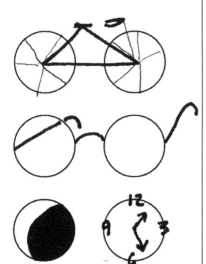

Additional rules

Do not repeat any drawings (i.e. only one drawing of a ball).

If your students can fill up the 20 circle easily then do twenty more. Do as many as you can without repeating any pictures.

Encourage your students to produce a variety of different types of objects.

Variation

You can do this activity using different shapes such as squares, ovals and triangles.

RORSCHACH

The images in your mind are the most powerful

Step #1   Get a piece of paper for each player and washable paint of any color.

Step #2   Have the students fold their piece of paper into two halves. Open the page and place a small amount of paint in the middle of the fold. Once again fold the paper so the paint is trapped inside. Open up the paper.

Step #3   Get into pairs. Have the students look at their pair's image that were created by the paint. Each alternately states a different thing the images can be until the fun is gone.

Images and what they can be

Hints

Use different color paints.

Have each player find at least five different things the image can be.

Encourage detail when describing the images.

You can title the image instead of describing it.

CONNECT THE DOTS

Dot-to-dot creations

Step #1   Have each student put several dots on a piece of paper, and then pass it to their right (or left) so that they get a different paper.

Step #2   With a pen, pencil or marker, your students connects all the dots, and then imagine what image the connected dots could be (a scene, object or ?). The players describe the image and name it.

Step #3   Continue the above for as often as you wish.

Examples of drawings

Tips

Start out with the first drawing using only a few dots and gradually increase the number of dots you put on the page.

Accept all drawings. Beware not to critique the quality of the drawing or whether the drawing looks like what it is intended to be (e.g. if your student says the drawing to the left is a guitar, accept it)

SERIAL DRAWING

Drawing a person

Step #1   Have each student fold a piece of paper into 5 equal horizontal parts.

Step #2   Starting from the top of the paper (in the first part) , the first person draws a head & neck of a person (man, child, or women), then folds this part over so that only just the bottom of the neck shows, and then passes to the next person.

Step #3   The next person draws the next part of the body: the neck to the waist. S/he then folds that sections of the paper and passes to the next person. This next person draws the waist to the knees, folds and passes to the next person who draws the knees to the ankles, folds and passes and lastly the feet are drawn.

Step #4   The completed drawing is shown to everyone.

Sample of paper fold

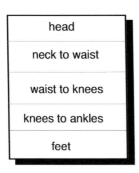

| head |
| neck to waist |
| waist to knees |
| knees to ankles |
| feet |

Hint

Make sure that the person receiving the next piece does not see the art segment before it. In other words, if you did the head, fold it over so the next person does not see the head you created.

Variation

You can do this with animals or other objects. Just divide it up into 5 discreet sections.

PICTURE THIS
Surmising & explaining pictures

Step #1   Collect interesting or even odd pictures. You can find them in magazines such as Life or National Geographic. Pick a picture.

Step #2   Have your students examine the picture and generate many different explanations (probable & improbable) for what is happening in the picture (without reading the captions). Imagine (out loud) what events happened that led to the scene in this picture.

Step #3   Pick another picture until you feel done.

Where to Find Pictures

* Magazines,
* Catalogs
* Posters,
* Gift books.

Variation

Think of an object, for example:
    Cane,
    Shoe,
    Pencil,
    Suitcase.
Then think of the object as broken. Ask how many ways could the object have broken?

Hints

Beware not to get into to the trap that the pictures must have a "real" explanation. The intent is not to find the real answer, but to play with ideas of explanation.

THIS-DOES-NOT-MAKE-SENSE

Explaining your sensory experiences using a different sense

Step #1   Fill in the blanks with the appropriate items:
- What does a [an item not usually associated with sound] **sound** like?
- What does a [an item not usually associated with smell] **smell** like?
- What does a [an item not usually associated with sight] **look** like?
- What does a [an item not usually associated with taste] **taste** like?
- What is the **texture** of a [an item not usually associated with touch]?

Step #2   Have all players alternate answering all the questions.

Step #3   Repeat steps #1 and #2 if desired.

Some examples

- What does a hot day sound like?
- What does the color purple sound like?
- What does wind taste like?
- What does a new idea sound like?
- What is the texture of happiness?
- What does happiness sound like?
- What is the texture of red?
- What is the sound of not being liked?
- What does the color blue taste like?
- What does a cloud smell like?
- What does a dog's bark feel like?

Hints

This task may be a bit difficult. In fact, the purpose is to push the players into thinking in new and different ways.

We are just not accustomed to mixing our senses. So be kind to your players if they respond with difficulty. Help them out without answering the questions for them, and do not judge their responses. This game can be extremely effective.

THIS MAKES A LOT OF SENSE
A variation of This-does-not-make-sense
Find sensations that are alike

Step #1   Fill in the blanks with the appropriate items:
What is another **sound** like the sound of [an item usually associated with sound]?
What is another smell like the **smell** of [an item usually associated with smell]?
What is another sight like the **sight** [an item usually associated with sight]?
What is a **taste** like the taste [an item usually associated with taste]?
What is a **texture** like the texture [an item usually associated with touch]?

Step #2   Have all players alternate answering all the questions. Go around as many times as you wish.

Step #3   Repeat steps #1 and #2 if desired.

Examples

* What is another sound like the sound of bubbling soda?
* What is another sound like the sound of chewing bubble gum?
* What is a smell like the smell of cherry pie?
* What is a taste like the flavor of a cinnamon?
* What is a texture like the texture of sand paper?
* What is a sight like the sight of a beautiful rose?

Hints

Make sure that you accept all responses. Never say a rose doesn't smell like a deck of cards! If the players say a rose smells like a deck of cards then it does (for the purposes of this game, anyway).

BODY SCULPTURING
Designing the human body

Step #1   Choose who will be the clay. The other person(s) will be the sculptor(s).

Step #2   The sculptor carefully moves the parts of the clay (body) to create any feeling, design or position.

Step #3   Alternate roles

How to sculptor a body

Move legs and arms in and out, up or down.
The body can be sitting or standing, knelling or on one leg.
Twist the body to the left or to the right.
Change the face: make it smile or frown.
Fingers need to be shaped too.
Do you want someone to hold something?
What direction do you want the head to face? Up, down, to the right or left?

Hints

Try many different positions.

For a little extra fun you may wish to name the sculpture.

Have fun!

SIMON DOES NOT SAY
An exercise in non-conformity

Step #1　　This game is just like Simon Says only you do the action when Simon doesn't say to do. So pick someone to go first to be "Simon."

Step #2　　That person directs the others to do something by just stating whatever there is to be done. When the person says "Simon Says..." and a person does it they are out of the game.

Things to do

* Touch parts of the body
* Touch another person
* Walk a certain way
* Say something

Hints

The faster you do this game the harder it is. Often though, kids need the challenge of a high-speed game or else you will be doing the game all day with no winner.

Allow everyone to have the chance to play "Simon."

FUNNY SILLY FACES

Let your hair down on this one: be wild, crazy and uninhabited. Kids love this!

Step #1   Go into pairs. Select "A" and "B." Have "B" go first. Ask "B" to a funny face at "A."

Step #2   "A" makes a different funny face to "B."

Step #3   "B" makes another funny face, but it must be different than all the preceding faces.

Step #4   Continue making funny faces, taking turns. Stop when the funny faces start repeating themselves. The object is to see how long your students can go without repeating a face.

How to make a funny faces

* Stick your tongue out
* Use your fingers
* Use your feet
* Use objects in the room
* Squeeze your cheeks
* Change your hair
* Use different emotional expressions
* Look in different directions
* How about your ears?
* Teeth can go in or out?
* Eyes can be crossed
* Use air in your mouth?

Hints

You can use props.

Think of different characters (clowns, politicians, relatives, cartoons, etc.)

Beware of laughter!

ACTING OUT...SILENTLY
A dramatic challenge

Step #1   Think up interesting activities for your students to pantomime. Write them down on a separate sheet of paper.

Step #2   Ask for a volunteer to go first (or use a lottery system). That student then picks on the sheets of paper and acts out the activity without words.

Step #3   The others guess what the student is doing.

Step #4   The person that guesses gets to go next. Do this until everyone has had a turn or you all had enough.

Ideas to Act Out

Without using words, act out a hippo following an ant into a manhole.

Without using words, pretend you have an itch in a place you cannot reach.

Without using words, act out a farmer whose donkey won't move.

Without using words, act out your favorite animal.

Hints

Do not worry about the situation or activity that you have chosen. The important thing is the challenge of doing something foreign to us.

You want your students to find a way to express him/herself freely in this activity. It is best when they feel that they can act silly and freely. The best way to invite free behavior is to model this behavior yourself. Get silly! Be a ham!

A CHANCE TO ACT OUT

Acting out your creativity

Step #1   All the players take a shopping bag and searches for three or more objects and places them in the bag.

Step #2   Exchange bags.

Step #3   Decide who goes first. That player must use the given props in a short play they make up on the spot

Step #4   The next player who has not acted must then use his/her given props to make up a new play. This is done until each player has a chance to act.

Props to get for the play

* Hats
* Clothes
* Umbrella
* Cookware
* Fake Telephone
* Stuffed animals
* Toys
* Eye glasses
* Candle
* Makeup
* Book
* Ball
* Flag

Tips

Encourage your students to get props that are very different from each other. In other words, if the students gets a pie tin then discourage him/her to also get a cake pan.

Variation

Have two people create a play together using their combined props. A good rule to reduce chaos is that actors only use their own props.

COMEDY WARS
JEST FOOLING, BUFFOONERY BATTLE
Go ahead, make 'em laugh

Step #1 Divide your group into two teams (its okay if the teams are uneven or if there is a team of one). Decide which team goes first.

Step #2 The first team does everything in their power to make the other team laugh. The only catch is that **you cannot touch the other team** (no tickling). So you have to rely on your physical and verbal wit.

Step #3 When each person on the receiving team laughs, switch places.

Things to do to get the other team laughing

* Make funny faces
* Tell a joke
* Remind the person of something they think is funny
* Stare into an opponent's face
* Walk funny
* Talk funny
* Say something serious in a non-serious way; say something non-serious in a serious way.

Hints

Should your student not be able to make others laugh help him/her to think of ways to make others laugh.

ANIMAL PLAY
Showing the animal in you

Step #1   Decide who goes first. (If this is the first time you play this game it is best for you to go first.) That person decides on an animal, and then starts to act like the animal.

Step #2   The others guess what animal it is. The animal imitator should not give any verbal hints.

Step #3   Switch roles

Animals Ideas

* Chimpanzee
* Elephant
* Otter
* Eagle
* Vulture
* Zebra
* Porcupine
* Hamster
* Donkey
* Python
* Lizard
* Alligator
* Spider

Hints

Have your animal do different things: walk, eat, play, lie and play.

IN THE MANNER OF THE ADVERB

Acting to express meaning...Asking pointed questions

Step #1 Decide on an "it." It goes out of hearing distance from the other players.

Step #2 The players decide on an adverb (any word that ends with "**ly**," like "Slowly").

Step #3 "It" is asked to come back to the group and asks each person, one at a time, to "do [something] in the manner of the adverb." The something should be specific. The player who is spoken to by the "it" does what is asked only in the manner of the adverb.

Step #4 Each time "it" asks someone to do something "It" guesses what the adverb can be. Continue until "It" guesses the picked adverb.

Adverbs

Angrily, Happily, Watchfully, Hesitantly, Merrily, neatly, & Grouchily (you can make up adverbs).

Things "It" can ask of the players

"Sing the Star Spangled Banner in the manner of the adverb"
"Dance with someone in the manner of the adverb"
"Give me a hug in the manner of the adverb"
etc...

Tips

This is best played with 4 or more people, but may be played with just 2.

Use easy words at first and perhaps always for young children.

Encourage your children to answer "it" with a lot of enthusiasm and a great deal of acting.

Encourage the "It" to ask the players to do unusual and creative things.

"It" may ask 2 or more people to do something in the manner of the adverb.

THIS AIN'T PEANUTS

Find your peanut among many...how sensitive are you?

Step #1   Put the same number of peanuts in a brown paper bag as you have players (the more players the better).

Step #2   All players pick one peanut out of the bag. The players are not to look at the peanut but are to feel it with their hands. The players explore their peanut until they think they know it. Then put it back in the bag.

Step #3   Pass the bad around and have all the players find their own peanut (again without looking).

Other objects you might use

* Walnuts
* Erasers
* Figurines
* Rocks
* Small toys

Tips

Make sure no one sees the object.

CHANGE

Observing what has changed

Step #1   Get into pairs. Select an "A" and "B." "B" goes first (or "A").

Step #2   "B" and "A" turn around so they cannot see each other. "B" then changes four things on them. It could be clothing, jewelry, hair, etc.

Step #3   The players turn around so the pairs can see each other. "A" then guesses what that "B" changed.

Step #4   Then reverse roles.

Things to change

* Take off a belt
* Comb your hair differently
* Put a ring on a different hand
* Change position of your glasses
* Put your watch on a different wrist
* Put a sock inside out

Once everyone figures out how to play the game, make the changes more subtle (less exaggerated).

Hints

Increase or decrease the number of "changes" to make it more or less difficult. For example, change only two things to make it easier or change six things to make it more difficult.

Give the players ample amount of time to guess the changes.

DID YOU HEAR ABOUT...

Guess what you are hearing

Step #1   Give each person a paper sack. All players gather together things that make sounds. The players should not show the others what they gathered...have them then place them in the paper sack to hide the objects.

Step #2   A person is selected. All the other players closed their eyes while the selected person takes out their object and makes sounds with it.

Step #3   The blinded players guess what object made the sound. Continue making the sound until a player guesses correctly or until "Uncle" is called.

Step #4   Switch roles.

Things to makes sounds

* Pots and pans
* Pencils and pens
* Paper ruffling
* Ruler
* Scissors
* Scratch surfaces
* Shoes banging
* Towels
* Zippers
* Knobs

Hints

You can use most any object to create most any sound, but find objects that will create sounds that are not too easy to figure out. Make it a little bit challenging and try to stump the other person.

WHAT IF...

Exploring possibilities and their consequences

Step #1   Select someone to go first.

Step #2   The first person thinks up a what if question starting with: "What would happen if (an unusual thing happens)."

Step #3   The other players go around and provide one answer each. Until everyone has a chance to answer the question.

Step #4   A new person is selected and repeats the above steps until everyone has had a chance to ask a "what if" question.

Examples of "What Ifs"

What would happen if we humans all had eyes behind our heads?

What would happen if we all were born with all we need to know?

What would happen if it were sunny all the time?

What would happen if you found a magic unicorn?

What would happen if you woke up in the morning and found that nobody was left on earth except you and someone you do not like?

Hints

Make sure you do not get into the "reality trap"— any "what if" is fine to use. It can be "crazy" or more "reality-based".

Encourage your students (and yourself) to find several (perhaps five or more) answers to a given "what if" question.

Encourage all players to withhold judgment of other's answers or "what ifs." All answers are acceptable as long as there is a connection to the question.

We recommend an adult to go first to model the activity.

ANY QUESTIONS?

All great ideas, inventions & discoveries start with a question

Step #1　　Think of a somewhat unusual question to ask your students.

Step #2　　Ask your students the question. The student each answer even if it is made-up.

Step #3　　Pick a student to ask another unusual question. The class responds with their answers.

Step #4　　Continue this until all students had a chance to ask a question.

Bizarre and unusual questions	Hints and suggestions
What is larger: an elephant or your smile? How fast can a kiss go? Why is red, red? What can go up and up? Do you like the bottom or the top of things more? What is louder a rock n'roll band or anger? When is it best to be happy? How do you feel the way you do? How do birds keep time? What is smoother: a lake or a baby's behind?	Remember to ask any question that comes to mind. The main lesson in this game is that there is no such thing as a stupid question. To make it easy to ask the first question that comes to mind, do not judge whether you can get a good answer from it or not. Remember: the questions listed here are just examples. Come up with your own ideas.

WHY?

Practice in conjecturing and developing theories

Step #1 Choose a fact, any fact. For example: Reality shows are getting more and more popular

Step #2 Ask your students: "Why do you think this is so?"

Step #3 Your students each answer the question.

Step#4 Let a student ask a similar question, and repeat steps #1-3

Examples of "what ifs"

Most people live in a house. Why do you suppose this is so?

Old fad and fashions seem to come back in style. Why do you think this is so?

Why do you suppose vanilla, chocolate, and strawberry ice creams are best sellers?

Music was invented. Why do you suppose this is so?

Hints

Use silly facts like "pigs don't have wings, why do you suppose this is so?"

Encourage your students to find more than one reason for the fact. Remember that the idea is not to find the truth of the matter but to stimulate thinking.

This activity works best with children over the age of 8.

WHY, WHY, WHY IS IT SO?

The constant "why" questions help us focus on getting answers

Step #1   Pick an event that is true or not

Step #2   Tell your students about this event and conclude by asking "Why did this happen?"

Step #3   Pick a student to answer the why question, and she/he too ends the reason by asking, "Why is this so?" That student picks another student to answer the question.

Step #4   The next student answers your question. This continues (repeating step #3) until the students are tired of asking and answering the why questions.

Examples of true & untrue events

* The faucet is leaking
* I am happy today
* King Kong ate a rose while walking to the library
* I once danced the watusi while crossing the Brooklyn Bridge

Hints

Remember to stick to the why question and its answer. Do not consider the accuracy of the answer, whether real or unreal.

Example of Game

Adult: I once danced the watusi while crossing the Brooklyn Bridge. Why do you suppose this is so?
Student#1: Because you entered a watusi contest that was held on the bridge. Why is this so?
Student #2: You entered the contest because you were looking for something new to do. Why do you think this is so?
Student#3 : Because you do mostly old stuff. Why?
Student #4: Because you have responsibilities
....and on and on

WHERE DO YOU SEE YOURSELF IN...

Bringing more control into ones life by thinking about the future

Step #1

Have the students get into pairs. Have them select who is an "A" and who is a "B." "A" asks of "B": "What do you think you will do tomorrow?" B answers.

Step #2

They switch roles and have "B" ask the above question to "A". "A" answers it.

Step #3

Have your students repeat the above but increase the time limit asked each time: one week, two weeks, one month, 6 months, 1 years, 5 years, etc.

Areas to envision for the future

* School
* Career
* Hobbies
* Parents
* Friends
* Vacations
* Education
* After School Activities
* Clothes
* Toys
* Values
* Religion
* Family

Hints

Encourage your students to talk about as many parts of his/her life as possible. The list on the left gives suggestions.

Make sure you or anyone do not judge your students' answers (even if s/he says she wants to be a garbage collector).

I WISH...

Dreams comes from a wish; Dreams are goals with wings

Step #1 First person picks a category, such as food.

Step #2 The others each come up with things they wish regarding this category (e.g. I wish I had a huge chocolate cake oozing with fudge right now).

Step #3 The next person picks a new category and then the others answer as before. Continue this until everyone gets a turn to provide one or more category.

Category ideas

* Sports
* Gardening
* School/work
* Homework
* Play
* Vacation
* Transportation
* Electronics
* Entertainment
* Art
* Decoration
* History
* Future

Tips

Encourage your students to get come up with things they really wish for, no matter how silly or "dumb" they may seem.

FANTASIA
Challenge each other's ability to fantasize

Step #1 Divide the class into teams of 3. Have them decide who will be "A," "B," and "C."

Step #2 "A" decides on a type of fantasy and begins by starting to create out-loud a fantasy. Introduce who the characters are and the context. Allow for about 2 minutes.

Step #3 The next person, "B" continues the fantasy for about 2 minutes, and introduces a problem or conflict situation.

Step #4 The last person, "C" gets 2 minutes to complete the fantasy and resolve the problem.

Step #5 Change roles as desired.

Fantasies

* Science fiction
* Fairy tale,
* Animal,
* Here & now

Some problems

A monster comes and destroys your property

The hero came upon a golden castle but could not find a way in.

Tips

You can change the timing to longer or shorter minutes, but make sure you decide on the time before you start the game. You can clock the game with an egg timer or a game timer from another game you may have around the house.

TWENTY QUESTIONS

Practice in asking focused questions and deducing

Step #1   A player is selected and thinks of a person or object without telling the other players.

Step #2   The other players take turns asking up to 20 "yes or no" questions to guess the object or person.

Step #3   The chosen player answers the questions stating only **"Yes,"** **"No,"** or **"I don't know."** The person who guesses the object or person wins (not that that is important).

Easy person or object

* A pencil
* A book
* A specific parent

Difficult person or object

* The sky
* Telephone poles
* An historical person

Hints

You may need to provide younger children with guidance as to what questions to ask: They (and some adults) have a tendency to want to guess an object immediately. Encourage them to ask broad and useful questions before they get to the 20th question.

MY FAVORITE THINGS
Looking at what you like from a different perspective

Step #1   Think of an object that your student's typically like. The goal is to guess the object by giving negative clues.

Step #2   Give a clue that expresses a negative aspect of the object. See below (left) for examples.

Step #3   The students guess what the object could be.

Step #4   When someone guesses the object that person then repeats steps #1-3.
.

Some favorite things and their negatives

Ice cream: Fattening, melts, gets sticky, too cold in the winter time, too many flavors to choose from...

Roses: They die when cut, need watering, have thorns, expensive to buy, some people are allergic...

Dogs: They die, hair gets all over the place, they have to be fed, can mess-up the house...traipse mud in it, can get lost...

Tips

When searching for negative statements for clues, think about all aspects of the object.

Concentrate on the process of developing clues and finding answers, not the answers themselves. In other words, winning is not important.

INVENTING & DESIGNING ACTIVITIES

Additional Activities you can do with your students

Invent...

- Invent a new flavor of any food: cereal, sandwich, ice cream, pizza, gum.

- Invent a new kind of musical instrument using the materials in your own home. Play music together.

Design...& Draw & tell about it

- Design your own dream house, school.

- Design a homework machine

- Design a new hair style

- Design a future perfect city

- Design a perfect teacher (or student)

- Redesign the classroom and actually carry it out if you can.

- Make a group drawing. Together make one big picture.

- Put on some music that all of you like, and do a dance with drawing or painting.

- Gather together several materials such as string, masking tape, rubber bands, and paper. Create something out of it.

DREAMS, SENSING & FUTURE ACTIVITIES

Additional activities you can do with your child

Dreams...

- Share your night-dreams together.

- Share your daydreams and fantasies together.

Sensory Experiences

- Everyone collects non-sharp items in a brown paper bag, without each other seeing what was put in the bags. Everyone take turn to guess what is in the bag by just touching the item. Use feathers, brushes, plants, cloth, cotton etc.

- Gather together a variety of tastes (for example, apples, oranges, cheeses, carrots, pudding etc.), and smells (for example, lemon juice, mint, cinnamon, sage, rose, burnt candle etc.). Blindfold you're the student and give them a sample of each. Slowly taking in each sensation one at a time.

- Go on a blindfold walk together. With one person being blindfolded and the other person leading go on a walk.

Look into the future

- Write a newspaper of the future. Put in articles you would like to see written. It can, and probably should, include personal as well as worldly news.

PROBLEMS, PASSIVE, PLANNING & FANTASY ACTIVITIES
Additional activities you can do with your child

Pose a Problem

- Pose a real-life problem about the world, the local government or the school to your students. Ask: "What might you do about...(the problem)?" Ask your students to find six possible answers. Instead of judging the answers build on them.

- Create a class "bug list" together. List things that bug you about anything (you, your friends, your house, your school/work, your city, your country, your world).

Active Passivity

- While reading a book to your students stop at appropriate spots and ask: "What might happen to... (The main character)?"

- While watching a video ask questions about how the plot of the story might turn out or what would your students do if they were in the same predicament as the character.

- Cut out a cartoon drawing from a newspaper and erase or cut out the captions. Create new captions.

Create Events

- Do something you and your students have never done before. Eat a new kind of food, go to a new place, experience a new activity, etc.

- Trade places for a day. You do your students work/activities. And your students do yours.

☝ Have mystery day where only one person knows what is going to happen. It is best if it is something really special. The point is to surprise your students.

☝ Plan a theme party together.

☝ Plan a field trip together.

☝ Do a creative scavenger hunt. The object is not to find the usual things like a ball of string, or a 45 record, but to search for unusual things such as something that looks like you, something soft, a relic of the past, something scary, a hiding place, something free, something that can't be photographed, etc.

☝ Have a complete day of silence where the class has to find ways to communicate without talking.

Guided Fantasy

☝ Do guided fantasies together. These are made-up fantasies that have a lot of imagery in them. Either read one from the guided fantasy books listed on page 92 or create one.

☝ Give each other imaginary surprises or gifts. Tell a story around the gift what it looks like, and how it came to be. Tell the story as if it is real.

Make-up...

🖐 Make up a slogan of your favorite soda pop, or candy

🖐 Make up a song about something you like

🖐 Make up a dance to some music

🖐 Make up a TV commercial for your favorite item.

Other Ideas

🖐 Interview each other as if the students are reporters on a newspaper.

RESOURCES FOR MORE INFORMATION & ACTIVITIES

All of these resources are recommended. The ones with a ℣ in front are highly recommended.

BOOKS

Stimulating and Nurturing Creativity

℣ **Awakening Your Child's Natural Genius**, by Thomas Armstrong, Ph.D. Jeremy P. Tarcher, 1991.

Brain Games! : Ready-to-Use Activities That Make Thinking Fun for Grades 6 – 12, Jossey-Bass, 2002

Frames of Mind: The Theory of Multiple Intelligence, by Howard Gardner. Basic Books, 1985.

Growing Creative Kids (Seeds for Success Series) by Evelyn Petersen, Totline Publications, 1997

℣ **Growing Up Creative: Nurturing a Lifetime of Creativity,** by Teresa M. Amabile, Crown Publishers, New York. 1989

Kids Who Think Outside The Box: Helping Your Unique Child Thrive In A Cookie-Cutter World, American Management Association, 2005

Parents' Guide to Raising a Gifted Child: Recognizing and Developing Your Child's Potential, by James Alvino and the editors of Gifted Children Monthly. Little, Brown, 1985.

Puzzles & Games for Critical and Creative Thinking (Gifted & Talented Workbooks) by June Bailey, Lowell House, 1994

Raising a Creative Child: Challenging Activities and Games for Young Minds, by Cynthia MacGregor, Replica Books, 1999

Teaching Creative Behavior: How to evoke creativity in children of all ages by Doris Shallcross, Prentice-Hall, New Jersey, 1981

The Do It Yourself Lobotomy: Open Your Mind to Greater Creative Thinking, by Tom Monahan, Wiley, 2002

The Joys and Challenges of Raising a Gifted Child, By Susan K. Golant, M.A. Prentice-Hall, 1991.

The Passionate Mind: Bringing Up an Intelligent and Creative Child, by Michael Schulman. The Free Press, 1991.

Thinking Games to Play With Your Child: Easy Ways to Develop Creative and Critical Thinking Skills, by Cheryl Gerson Tuttle, Penny Hutchins Paquette, Lowell House, 1991

Inventing

Steven Caney's Invention Book, Workman Publishing, New York, 1985

The Unconventional Invention Book: Classroom Activities for Activating Student Inventiveness by Bob Stanish, Good Apple, 1981

Problem Solving

☞ **The Book of Think (or How to Solve A Problem Twice Your Size**), By Marilyn Burns, A Brown Paper School Book, 1976

Guided Fantasies

☞ **Put your Mother on The Ceiling: Children's Imagination Game**, by Richard De Mille, Penguin books, 1973.

Scamper, by Robert Eberle, Prufrock Press, 1971.

Coloring Activities

☞ **The Anti-Coloring Books, The Second Anti-Coloring Book** and **The Third Anti-Coloring Book** all by Susan Striker with Edward Kimmel, Owl Books,

PERIODICALS

Creative Child and Adult Quarterly. National Association for Creative Children and Adults,

☞ **FamilyFun**, monthly magazine Family Fun Magazine

Gifted Child Quarterly. National Association for Gifted Children.

The Gifted Child Today..

Creative Kids, Written by and for children ages eight to eighteen.

ONLINE SHOPPING

www.thinkbutton.com, Knowledge Products for Growing Minds

www.creativekidsunlimited.com, Creative Kids Unlimited- Award-winning educational toys and learning games for Children.

www.ideashoppe.net, Toys and tools for the creative mind

ONLINE

www.innovationtools.com provides resources on innovation, creativity and brainstorming

www.creativepuzzels.nl, Puzzles

www.archimedes-lab.org, provides puzzles and mental activities

www.enchantedmind.com

www.mycoted.com Creativity and innovation in science

www.ideaguides.com Consulting firm devoted to facilitation of collaborative creative activity

ASSOCIATIONS

Creative Education Foundation.
www.creativeeducationfoundation.com

To Order This Book Online

Go to www.ideaguides.com/book.html or
e-mail aha@ideaguides.com

1. **Have a game you wish to share**? We would love to hear about them. If we publish it we will send you a **free game**.

2. **Found an error**? Is there an error spelling, grammar, or formatting? If we agree with your correction we will send you a **free game**.

3. **Don't understand any of the instructions?** Ask us and well make it clearer?

4. **Got any comments or ideas?** We would love to hear from you!

Write to us at aha@ideaguides.com

ABOUT THE AUTHOR

Bruce E. Honig...

has been a creativity and innovation specialist for over 25 years. Bruce's **Masters of Education** at the University of Oregon was focused on the **psychology of creativity**.

Bruce is an author of several articles and two other books on creativity: **Aha! A Workbook in solving problems, Creative Collaboration: Simple Tools for Inspired Teamwork** (Crisp publications)

He is the inventor of **CREATE: The Game That Challenges and Expands Your Creativity** a board game, as well as 4 other games involving using ones creative muscles for various ages: **Sproin-n-g, Idea Factory, Choices** and **Just Imagine.**

Bruce was... a producer and creator of **Brainstormers** a game show where the contestants compete for their ability to brainstorm, a publisher and editor of **The Creative Mind Newsletter: : A Guide to Innovation & Creativity in Business...& Life**, and the creator of "Games for Creativity," A workshop where games were used to stimulate and provoke creative action.

Made in the USA
San Bernardino, CA
15 December 2015